Disappearing by the Math

"We are dogs who love their morning walks but not their names"
~ *Jim Harrison*
(In Search of Small Gods)

Disappearing by the Math

Disappearing by the Math

by

Matt Thomas

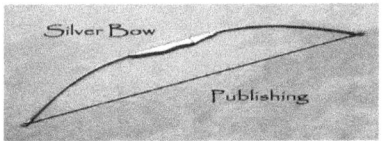

720 – Sixth Street, Box # 5
New Westminster, BC
V3C 3C5   CANADA

Title: Disappearing by the Math
Author: Matt Thomas
Publisher: Silver Bow Publishing
Cover Art: "Attack From Space" painting by Candice James
Layout/Design/Editing: Candice James

All rights reserved including the right to reproduce or translate this book or any portions thereof, in any form without the permission of the publisher. Except for the use of short passages for review purposes, no part of this book may be reproduced, in part or in whole, or transmitted in any form or by any means, either by means electronically or mechanically, including photocopying, recording, or any information or storage retrieval system without prior permission in writing from the publisher.

ISBN: 978-1-77403-288-6 paperback
ISBN: 978-1-77403-289-3 e- book

© Silver Bow Publishing 2024

Library and Archives Canada Cataloguing in Publication

Title: Disappearing by the math / by Matt Thomas.
Names: Thomas, Matt (Author of Disappearing by the math), author.
Identifiers: Canadiana (print) 20240293401 | Canadiana (ebook) 2024029355X | ISBN 9781774032886
  (softcover) | ISBN 9781774032893 (Kindle)
Subjects: LCGFT: Poetry.
  Classification: LCC PS3620.H6575 D57 2024 | DDC 811/.6—dc23

Disappearing by the Math

For Chelle and Aut

Disappearing by the Math

Contents

Buddha Lesson / 9
Trespass / 10
Smoke Break, M Street, September / 11
Summer Scar / 12
I Yelled at You Because the Dog is Old / 13
This Poem is Not About Killing a Rooster / 14
Marcescence / 15
Nude Descending a Staircase / 16
I Can't Stop Imagining Your Death /17
Still Life at the P.O. / 18
Now That We've Been Shepherds of our Data / 19
The Fall Cords / 20
Compass / 21
Tangibles / 22
Buddy / 23
Dentist / 24
The Folks / 25
Bird Dogs / 26
Linden / 27
September 1st / 28
On This Day in 2003 / 29
Arts and Crafts / 30
A Natural History / 31
The Hands of Purpose / 32
Two Snows / 33
House Carpenter / 34
Eagle Head / 35
Kineograph / 36
In Which You Are Hit by a Rocket / 37
The Graffiti Artists / 39
White '76 TR7 / 42
Warp / 43
Japanese Ice-Cream / 44
Every Shelter in Place / 46
Snail Rider / 47
Slow Boat / 48
A Theory / 49

A Response to Pablo Neruda / 50
Starting Over / 51
The Songwriter / 52
To Loneliness / 53
Sensitive Boy / 54
Linear Decrease / 55
Self Harm at the Outlet Mall / 56
Goldfinch / 57
My Father Paints Us a New Car / 58
The Phenomena / 59
Hides / 60
Open Carry / 62
For Albert Hawkins / 63
Golden Boys / 64
Lover / 65
Yield / 66
Pop Song / 67
When You Stretch I / 68
Dressed for the Flood / 69
Idiom / 70
The Unknown / 71
Fetch / 72
Every Morning Song / 73
Rosslyn Plaza / 74
Naturalization / 75
Give / 76
Banyan / 77
Canopy Shyness / 78
Solving for X / 79
Fire Break / 81
What/Nothing / 82
True Romance / 83
Yellow Boy / 84
Atlas / 85

Acknowledgments . 88
Author Profile / 89

Buddha Lesson

A ginger cat paused in the middle of the road
watching my oncoming car and then,
sensing my intent to turn left, sat,
began chewing at a claw in tune, somehow,
with life and death.

That was driving to work.

Driving home I was angry, stopped in traffic.
I watched an old woman eat a sandwich on a bench,
hospital-blue mask slung beneath her jaw,
no longer for COVID but for the wildfire smoke,
starling'd cheeks sucking and blowing,
chewing with molars and then incisors,
reaching the tip of her tongue to clean her lips
not demonstrating particular joy or bother,
her hair seamed in back with a plain barrette,
the kind sold in ten packs
as impulse buys at CVS.

I joined her mind in that nap of a space between
the completion of a chore
and the countdown to its repetition
yawning into my circumstance as a swallow,
at least for that moment
which made me think also of birds,
and so cats.

Trespass

Tell me what it is about age
that urges you to buy a handheld leaf blower
and systematically eradicate the leaves
from every corner of the lawn.
Is it because a lawn is a ridiculous idea
and irritated at having served it a lifetime
you follow its care now to the letter
or, being positive how
the barbed wire held aside
to allow you to step through
down coat flagged with feathers
poking from the care
you are disinterested in showing yourself
is not spite but trespassing,
when there are leaves
accruing on the grass at home;
a trade, age about its own,
white coil jutting from wet dark
like the belly of a salamander or snake
waiting out the cold beneath?

Smoke Break, M Street, September

Reflected by water tensed on the horizontal,
waxy petals of rootless slumping Fall pansies
Passing time hand to mouth
as St. Matt's rings the quarter hour
Bulging, distorted, ash-flecked, huddled molecules
Pacing, flickering. Wildly thrown light
casting a bind at each toll,
stretching the membrane of the moment.

Between each dripped note, an exhale at a time,
pyrolysis, everyday magic
Roughing lungs to take the paint
of the shape of our escape
Sketches in quick strokes
on grids of need, pale as the sky's worn bluing
Each line like the brush of a starling wing:
a Kiss with a little bit of tongue,
shotgun, for the sagging afternoon,
the cherry trees
half-naked questioning the mirror.

Summer Scar

A hanging flower basket swings.
The cedar scent of a rat snake
flicks a tongue at the rain.
To the west a hematoma
        in time lapse pools
while heat, propped on an elbow,
unkempt, reclines.

A close talker, he inches
like a little green worm
        up my shin;
an itch that is thankfully silenced
at the healed numb ridge
of a remembered ruined moment:

hurt, calqued. Better than ice.
Like a ball of Yellowjackets
frozen on the comb.
I use it to soothe
the back of my neck, my throat.

Was it a trip and fall running
        or a bicycle?
It usually is.

You have the same —
yours a little higher toward the knee —
a thin white finger hushing
summer's limp flagged temptation
to lengthen the day,
see everything as the same
rather than common.

I Yelled at You Because the Dog is Old

You both distrust your bodies
and mince around underfoot;
accidents waiting to happen.

He was hurt that you would scold him
for existing the way he knows how
while doing the same.

I've never understood anyone's meanness
        but my own
so I yelled at him also,
to allow you to hear yourself.

While you
and he each made your way,
heads down, to the sofa,
I held your misery and his in the kitchen,
listening to the faucet drip;
the many things to fix,
none of which matter,
        I know,
but can't believe.

This Poem Is Not About Killing a Rooster

Eventually he leaned against the coop
panting, still defiant, watching
as if for an opening in the fight,
mirroring my own stare searching
for a seam or a verge,
the sharp spurred intuition
that sometimes feints at the face
        of a misjudged reach
and awards the consolation to look
where you've realized you left
the misplaced thing
while cleaning up the glass and milk.

Afterward,
his foot twitching like 'go on, go on,'
butterflies mistook him for a meal —
a common enough mistake —
as I went.

Marcescence

When the new leaves unroll,
the old won't be pushed aside
they cling, deflated brown balloons
in the green ruining the effect of life —
maybe protecting new growth,
or as a source of mulch in the spring —
an attractive idea
as I've been waiting to age into a baseline,
be fitted to a set of expectations
by the rules of a season.

It would be nice if the rattling
turned out to be functional
and not just a quirk of character;
the traps and falls of a parent
that every kid commits to memory,
mine unsticking her forehead from the window,
backhanding drool,
her entire self cupped, offered,
waiting for my face to open with the door.

And then, in a blast of summer heat,
aftershave and aching, pursed kindness,
accepting a bag of grease, dough, sugar
What I can do: proximate intimacy
between the jostling things I keep,
wake her on the road with donuts.
Repeatable, demonstrable proof
that my something to offer is worth wanting.
'Good?' asking
for a nod, a mechanical force
to clear the branches of the everciduous
possible outcomes,
allow me to trust the reliable nature
like as not,
of the current rotation and orbit.

Nude Descending a Staircase

It's natural to disbelieve what you were born knowing,
to spend life lipping things you know you can't eat

To slide a hand along the banister, studying
the strips hiding each join in the ceiling.

To focus on the nothing furred between stars, drywall;
the sense common to your gaps, everything missed,
got away and still able to reach back

To feel deeply for each way of living,
stuffing the cracks with whatever is at hand
against the draught of tongue lolling, pacing dog panic
that the fire alarm will ring at 2 am,
the burglar strobes activate,
the ice weighted tree collapse,
the airbags deploy

To feel affection in the rising smell of breakfast
toward your own bone and tendon,
imagine each knuckle a knot reminder
of the weight of your reliability

To consent to gravity, reaching fingers, toes,
blindly to pull the next step into your mouth
while gripping the guiding arm of stillness,
that worn smooth, fleshed name,
toward the sound of love's consonants, assonance,
ignoring the shards of movement

To leave the splinter when it comes,
a dark shaft of arrow in the meat
in case you're tempted, as I sometimes am,
to remember you're just a trick of the light.

I Can't Stop Imagining Your Death

Your ragged snores scoring the day losing seconds
like bright leaves shed onto black dirt
each breath snagged and restarted,
stubborn as the planet's inertia
and yet yours is not a friction-less existence
so I worry, sure, but that's not this,
this is playing your absence,
crying on cue tears that heat
the material of the present to impressionable goo
and stomping in the puddle of it.

It's harmless; no big deal.
Sometimes I imagine your death.
I'm not prescient. It's nothing.
I shouldn't have mentioned it.

It's just that in moments of transition, such as now,
sun setting, estranging the house and your breathing,
or when some unexpected light or cloud
disfigures a familiar road
and causes me to become momentarily, startlingly, lost,
I imagine you dying.

No different than thrilling at the wind
stirring dead leaves,
everything going to play
to steady the staggering present.

Still Life at the P.O.

In line at the post office, fluorescent light blinking,
each wink generating a low frequency pinging whine
over and over, which in seconds I assigned
as a reliable noise to the hesitant queue
approaching the steps of the process,
the next uncertain, physical interaction
clutching the something firing, firing,
corresponding with purpose at each inconvenience.

An oscillating fan wet the clerk's shirt to reveal his torso
as he worked blades broadcasting glue and rubber form
to the idea of the post, exchange of signs and meaning;
the eye of a body gazing from the packaging —
not firearms, not solvents — foodstuffs labeled, address affixed,
packed imagining the travel, delivery, reveal:

a bowl of fruit, two hanging birds, cheese and apples,
a half-drunk glass of wine: still life fluffed to an interest in you
on its way to something else. Valued by weight
of the accrued consumption encroaching hand to hand

on shuffling feet, horses, ships, planes, trucks;
wheezing bellows, starters cranking energy
station to station to threshold
of the other same as yours and a moment of decision

to allow inside (or not) the look you have arranged,
nestled in bubble wrap, greedy for the shaping light to share
with that foreign you who will concede that you were right
to send the meaningful thing
even though you don't know what it is
or why you suddenly, certainly had to love it.

Now That We've Been Shepherds of Our Data

A night bird like grey crayon on black paper
a shooting star after the fact burned out, tumbling thrown
underhand it seems strange that something would take off
with no coordinates for landing.
I have mine tapped into the nav system
tracking my progress down the gravel road
white as shell in the brights,
deer slinking in the bushes, raccoons surveying the road
from the high grass possums, foxes, cats,
sometimes dogs fucking.

All the creatures out and about, returning from or going to,
and you are home I'm certain shut down,
head tilted to the side in sleep mode waiting
for either light or motion to fire your servos,
cause a stretch and yawn.

We asked our students,
'Do robots dream of mechanical sheep?'
Now that we've been shepherds of our data we don't doubt,
the bleating a familiar haptic dynamic of our umwelt.

Apart from you it's these other actuating things
that calibrate my proprioception,
are the found devices of information in love with itself,
order painting with the soft pallet of chaos
until we pair again at the end of the driveway
sensing we're in range of our trues and falses.

The Fall Cords

Headlights carving an egress
through the soybeans
coming home with a load of drunk kids
back from my daughter's 21st birthday party
thrown without a hitch
as long as no one throws up in the truck.
The country snaking by, pasture,
trees and telephone poles,
what they'd have plowed into
had I not stayed sober
winning the easy points,
keeping my eyes on the road,
burning that gold star
to warm my optimism,
dread cocked like an ear,
remembering my father's hands on the wheel
same as she'll remember mine,
or another familiar thing
which will erase me, light
thrown on the road immediately in front,
disappearing by the math,
nothing but memory, imagination:
the bare firewood bin in June,
a claim without proof
that the Fall cords were.

Compass

All of the many chaoses
With their levers and springs
Cat skulls and pancake mushrooms
card games and twilights
All of the pennies stacked
Late braking, numb moments
in the shower waiting
for the comfort to be enough.
The fan oscillates, spraying
mutilated syllables,
warning off fingers,
having its say
same as the summer.

Cotton Mouth, Mepps spinner in the pink,
fangs like the driveway pillars
of the doctor's house we trespassed
for a bucket of panfish.
"Careful, he'll bite your pecker."
Reminded me of *pants*
same way first time I heard "fuck"
I thought *ferry boat*

I hug myself in my sleep beside
someone who would gladly do it for me
Sweating trespasses,
cutting lines of declination to watch
each loosed rope of meaning
skate the murk away
slick in the moon close mouthed
my hooks going to rust
in dandy high cotton.

Tangibles

It's an old cliche
about the wind being evidence
of the existence of things unseen
but watching the porch rocker keep time
from inside the stillness of the house
it seems obvious that the old analogy holds water
especially when, every day, our machines discover
some new limitation of our senses
so it's not even philosophical now
just plain fact
to say that the bulk of everything
happens unbeknownst
which maybe explains
the stubborn impulse to heaven
some place that,
based on the example of the wind,
surely exists
some place that we haven't thought up,
stunk up, tore up
where the magic of our imagination
has not stopped up
against the horror of our insignificance

Why I saddle that rocker with any number of names,
hoping for the kind of distracted touch
that sometimes happens while watching television
someone reaching for the dog
and instead stroking a leg,
conveying love
unseen during the day's argument

That energy
implying a source, not human made
the strike of wooden rails on stone
a thin, dead, hollowing thing knocking
at what may be the last to go

Compass

All of the many chaoses
With their levers and springs
Cat skulls and pancake mushrooms
card games and twilights
All of the pennies stacked
Late braking, numb moments
in the shower waiting
for the comfort to be enough.
The fan oscillates, spraying
mutilated syllables,
warning off fingers,
having its say
same as the summer.

Cotton Mouth, Mepps spinner in the pink,
fangs like the driveway pillars
of the doctor's house we trespassed
for a bucket of panfish.
"Careful, he'll bite your pecker."
Reminded me of *pants*
same way first time I heard "fuck"
I thought *ferry boat*

I hug myself in my sleep beside
someone who would gladly do it for me
Sweating trespasses,
cutting lines of declination to watch
each loosed rope of meaning
skate the murk away
slick in the moon close mouthed
my hooks going to rust
in dandy high cotton.

Tangibles

It's an old cliche
about the wind being evidence
of the existence of things unseen
but watching the porch rocker keep time
from inside the stillness of the house
it seems obvious that the old analogy holds water
especially when, every day, our machines discover
some new limitation of our senses
so it's not even philosophical now
just plain fact
to say that the bulk of everything
happens unbeknownst
which maybe explains
the stubborn impulse to heaven
some place that,
based on the example of the wind,
surely exists
some place that we haven't thought up,
stunk up, tore up
where the magic of our imagination
has not stopped up
against the horror of our insignificance

Why I saddle that rocker with any number of names,
hoping for the kind of distracted touch
that sometimes happens while watching television
someone reaching for the dog
and instead stroking a leg,
conveying love
unseen during the day's argument

That energy
implying a source, not human made
the strike of wooden rails on stone
a thin, dead, hollowing thing knocking
at what may be the last to go

Buddy

Once, in the gravel beside the beltway,
I saw what I thought was a struck deer
and my heart jumped,
though passing saw
that it was a cardboard box.
Still, my heart saw it as a deer.

This tourist balancing
her bike upright at an intersection
slowly pedaling backwards,
the sound of the sprockets clicking
clear over the radio in my car,
startles my heart past
the sweat curled edge of your bangs
to your eyes, laughing
taking a breather at a stop sign,
my friend,
a word to break your heart
pedaling backwards, not knowing,
thank god,
that we were having a moment.

Dentist

Locust leaves,
beyond the window
darkening and lightening
gloss to matte and back,
the pleasantly fat, bitter
latex'd fingers of the hygienist
harping my jaw,
breath inches from my own,
an intimacy
of saliva and suction, distress
and relief by the hand
of another was I remember,
my vanity, before
I ever thought
to whiten a tooth.

The Folks

Seung Sahn said, 'There are three types of killing:
our parents, the buddha, and our Selves.'

I can't kill you, prehistory, at the small, round,
chrome edged table centered in the room
entered through an arch, stove and door to the left,
refrigerator to the right, sink straight ahead.
The small conversational sounds
that reached my bedroom and seemed
at once distant and yet intimate:
a characteristic I intuited as unique to you
but would recognize later in a train whistle
or a mouse scrabbling in a wall.
You were children,
nothing but yourselves: no money, no philosophy,
time unburied, every day a scratch at ridiculous plans
fencing debt, low pay, no education.
I could bring myself to kill you,
but not to the killing moment
of losing you before you thought to close the house to summer,
glorious rot invited in on legs,
the hug of delicate, limp petalled wilt
behind doors, windows open to the robins.

Bird Dogs

For Bobby

Even as summer rises, green leaves rustling whetting their edges, I'm the inside of a fence stalking the out, a driver, too young to shoot, doves tearing through the husks as we marched, car alarms firing one at a time up the block, sun like an over-washed bedsheet above glances back over rolling shoulders at the crack of a shot, clack of the jaw of the dead. That changing air — cold eating through jeans into long underwear, taillights disappearing, breeze ticking the dried leaves twisted in place like frozen rags. Next day, Sunday, shared bed, Casey Kasem, smell of dog, chaff on the carpet. I still prefer to wake up that way, window open, dedicating songs to lost causes. You in the ground, me above it, same dirt. Keeping an eye on the driver beside me, maintaining the line & ceremony of our season.

Linden

Following the ricochet of sun around the kitchen
mistaking heat for warmth
like a wasp
lovelorn on a propane tank.

That's how I'm getting old,
flirting with the gas
in the only room of the house
where the seasons coexist.

Sometimes I drag a hand
nearer the latch each circuit;
sink to coffee maker,
coffee maker to table,
your sweater over the chair
as if you've dived into the floor
until, with barely a touch,
the door swings open behind me.

Obviously, I'm on the way out,
preferring the scrabble
and jump of wild grief
over the lick and shift of it in the crate, waiting.

September 1st

Is the gate closed?
The grader scrapes at the gravel road
in a cloud of blue dust.
Ironically, drought is beautiful,
raining mercury in twilight.
The road won't stay flat, wants
to bunch like carpet.
Open the window, let the flying ant out.
The dog is fine, she's bringing
cleavers into the house
seeds fallen
on the dead wood floor.

On This Day in 2003

Okra in a ball cap, sticky little horns,
    aping a rib
beneath the grub-soft spot
where her t-shirt has risen.

The baby cries, startles even the Jays,
air whistled between the blades of her and me.

Devil's Walking Stick ferries the wreck
of the fence we built
and bears destroyed
the same way it went up,
one horizon at a time, a story
I pitch out with a smile
and she turns and catches. It's humid;
no-see-ums itch the weeding.

We are salting every bane
in our garden of babies and birds
with sweaty intention,
held and re-nailed
each time more cleverly than before
to spite the Devil walking.

Arts and Crafts

Sometime last week,
clumps of orange twine blew from the back of a truck
and have been flowering on 66 East since then,
gusts from passing cars arranging them this way and that
each morning a surprise, although the color is fading.

I recorded 30 seconds of Lake Michigan while on vacation
that I play in my office; perch navigate orange bladderwort
below the wheeling cries of delivery trucks
backing into the alley behind the Jefferson.

People like to say Michigan resembles a mitten. It does,
in the way that gobs of string
describe the features of territories and states to come:
a lake chopped into snow fence,
clay under the nails of what has its way, twists
with that awful squeak into whatever needs be.

I've woken myself with a rough breath,
imagining a lashing storm,
ignoring the wonder of the mechanics of living for a sign.

Round about me, every face I've ever made:
lands bordered in orange twine, taut passages
plotted between pins hammered to have the sound.

A Natural History

Soon every time I found a bit of you
I'd hold that claw or feather and wait
for the cramp of appetite
you sensed was my true nature.
Sometimes I walked to the 7-11,
bought Chesterfield Kings and swaggered home,
tobacco in my teeth but by the door
I was a boy again,
runny nose, shedding his coat in the hallway,
the only thing I was able to shed,
while you molted for the umpteenth time.

I'd find your skin around the apartment in odd places:
a crumpled foot, half of a face;
once I found an antler, which felt lucky
but scared me, implied disquieting growth:
I was sure that one day I'd come home to the 50-foot woman.
When I took your hand while watching television
your bones in mine struck me as sticks covering a pit trap
while crows hawked atop the parking lot lights,
rips in the thin atmosphere peeping
the dark tangle of your habitat.

Watching you laughing,
tearing a similar hole in the sky stretched over Blue Mountain,
that story is a feature of the landscape I notice
but don't point out
while hurrying to find a seat before the music begins,
nearly every chair filled with sighing assigned names,
Sharpie on masking tape, a loopy, optimistic fail
at classifying the unexplained I promise
I'll look into your eyes when you talk
and take no notes, count not knowing that much
as a long way from when I knew nothing.

The Hands of Purpose

Incongruous as a pelican in a birch tree
but not astounding.
When you're taught to see nature as a gift
everything is:
the two headed toad,
the channel cut into the beachhead,
80 degrees in February,
you see purpose revealed in a May blizzard,
wonder of strange migratory birds
appearing at the feeder.

We've come this far riding elephants of adaptation:
the gruesome wreck,
the burned torso,
the underside of the overpass
stared at from a sour sleeping bag.
Rolling pasture,
columbine and cowbane
all kneading comfort:
the greater the devastation,
the more strident the hands of purpose.

Two Snows

It snows once, weighting the trees
the way that mergansers
weight cold-black water
and during that snow
it's dry beneath the cedars.
so much so you can lie
on the dead needles like a warm pallet
and watch the snow falling
until it doesn't land on you.

The second snow falls maybe a day
or a night later
and is a gentled snow
it falls heavy or soft
depending on the movement of the boughs
sifted fine it fills your collar
the seams of your jacket
shushing from the canopy
the small striking sound
of each grain lost
in the needles below.

Two snows and the Mergansers
who never leave their feathers to be found
in icy mud like Mallards or Geese,
that float light as sucked eggs,
like the mineral remnant
of every shamed, juxtaposed thing,
will never experience the second
which is for me, foxes, coyotes, deer,
wrens even,
those of us not buoyant or fastidious.
Drowners
given that gift as consolation.

House Carpenter

I heard it while taking my morning walk.
Some caught breath escaping the caulk, tar,
brought on the morning horseshoe crabs and glass.
Was it your voice?
More likely my own, the worst kind of leaver;
the kind that stays
and looks back from a distance.

Your picture on the refrigerator,
a wide salty smile
like a hand over the mouth of my apology.
I filled the ice trays
imagining the clunk of cubes sunken in a glass,
as the sound of you in the room above,
a vocalization of your drowned regret
passing between our separate environments.

So much of my translation is what I want to hear.
Why, that gray morning, in the quiet kitchen
I imagined your footsteps thumping down the stairs
to embrace domesticity, purge
the freedom from your lungs: an ocean
on the hardwood to learn to skirt
not walk into and out of it while making ice, dinner, love
as if it's not wet, your stubborn tracks, salt outlines
of where you're not — our world was not
a tidal pool, brief caught environment,
ours was a towering forest,
fresh water, no single axe or design
even now if the moon sucks stump teeth
if I fashion your voice from friction.

Eagle Head

For Kim

Unsharpened face
leaning toward the stone
pulling espadrilles over
wet feet distrusting the plan.
Wind tugs the dripping hem
of the bathing dress that you body
shapes contemptuously and
your sister's dog; one of
those things that they
teach you to want.

But I remember
you bursting from the old
dark and ivy'd barn like
a terrible thing woke
gripping mane in both
hands, riding the flailing heart.
I remember your knees
in the sweat, hair the proud
pennant of that closed country
before you were parted.

Kineograph

It's interesting how the right combination,
right bird call and right humidity, wind,
never anything obvious, always a level down, transplants
sense of season — Spring and Fall mostly
but sometimes, morning especially, Summer to Spring.

These moments your body configures itself momentarily
for that other set of expectations,
collapses inward or expands, bristles/softens,
oils summoned or suppressed,
microbiome shifted en masse to find the small advantage
of the conditions. You can feel it, the realignment,

same I imagine, as transmogrifying into a bird or bear
and then back, but in between a shimmer,
occupying two states of intuition,
a goosed flesh glimpse of a law usually hidden:
that everything must occur at once to occur at all.

Although winter is never anything
it is sometimes,
counterintuitively,
when I feel that shiver the most

as it's not happening

Same as I write best about heartache
when I'm happily in love
when I'm sure in the lie
that I'm one thing in turns

In Which You Are Hit by a Rocket

Your name is the first to go
even before the cheatgrass wilts
before the caterpillars are hurled
in their sod homes,
before the fungi'd stump
that you had bent to touch
disassembles, your body ruptures,
turns inside out cell by cell.

Before your toast, coffee, kiss at the door.
Before the parent who named you
first thought, "they'll be X," that's the moment
when your name sensed the detonation and fled,
that fast, no more a trick
than the solid transforming into a gas
so quickly as to demolish you.
Or the way your death occurs over infinite time
similar to the way you loved,
erecting the stubborn parts like stones
fitting the shapes together
in the way they spooned best,
allowing the shapes
to make the thing they always wanted to be
and you, the builder, were the numbered beats
of each of their satisfied stone hearts,
each unique like snowflakes
and each the same like star dust
which you always thought a gaudy, shameful analogy
but you held to regardless

Because what if

this entire existence is a tacky magic,
something even peeper frogs are born knowing.
Maybe the frogs call us sad as a noun
because our parasitic brains have walked us off
from that one known thing

Disappearing by the Math

that makes life worth the pain of rockets,
which of course it is,
because the rockets don't hit everyone.

But more fundamental

is that you did realize
that rain on a roof is a comfort
because you aren't getting wet
not because the sound is pleasant, though it is.

So the woo-woo of it aside, you stuck with the stardust;
otherwise there was no reason,
no purpose, no end game at all,
just accident, happenstance;
you'd been spit out by a blind luck machine;
a found dog, stolen street sign,
fallen limb, off-target rocket;
your life an iteration of semi-colons
and you died like you were created:
in a slap of skin, your only magic
the ability to comfort another.
To kiss. To hear a cat snore.
Or to stand on a hill at night
and see the lights of a city
like a bioluminescent spider web
on the grass of some dark hollow.
All of those souls or what have you, peeping in their spring.

But if a solid
can turn into a gas expanding
faster than a train
in the blink of an eye ...
if that's possible what isn't?
Surely the world and all of the life in it is a wonder,
which is what you were thinking
when you bent to look at the stump.

The Graffiti Artists

1

Derailed, the container cars, yawed
and stranded outside of context,
seemed beached,
the Norfolk-Southern salvage team
flensers working acetylene knives.

They cut carefully, so as not to shift the load
and cause the car to lurch,
like gas animating a corpse.

When the metal of the car exclaimed,
the crew became immediately still, listening.
This happened several times until
silently and with a terrible slowness,
a car ate them: fell,
jagged and gaping.

We watched, sweaty with agitation
as the car rocked and settled,
the orifice of it a smile
in the Queen Anne's Lace.

The crowd murmured and stepped back,
electing us,
hands in pockets, knotted and blind in the noise
of the explicitly stated,
poets to invent the name
for that winking, gross expression.

2

The creek had been just another boasting playmate
until it swore and rose
beardless and yet
having absorbed the support

of the beaded grasses, dripping cedars, boated catalpa
bulged, feeling a just discovered violence
when yesterday the worst it could do was leeches,
became aimless, terrifying to itself
spewing frogs, snakes, drowning wasps by the dozens.

Later, in the flooded boxcar, Penthouse magazines floated
    like butterflies.
We separated the pages
    with the patience of surgeons, minds like abattoirs.

We imagined we could smell the blood.

3

Part the thistles noting your hand,
how your parts catching you pre language
 summarize a revelation

Duck beneath yellow safety tape
cradling each grain of the sky
into the mouth blotting

Always in reserve
the things you forget
the moment after rescue
how you were certain
until unplaced,
grasshoppers pinging against the container
enunciating the trap, the jumped track

    the repaired ruin in the open casket, sparrows
    mapping the retreat of the flood,
    48,000 lbs. of LeSuer Very Young Sweet Peas
        dried to gravel, sown by the water above
        plowed under by the water below

    genitalia, penetralia

how we despaired the wrong word,

because the engine of the wind in the stilt grass,
because the come-along inching.

4

A fishy gut;
wood and cardboard in the dark.
Smell of sponge, fecund, multitude,
having absorbed so many things
as to exist simultaneously as everything

Three in the belly
"I felt a shove and then everything went black"
in their distress calling
leeching into the sponge

And we kids
witness,
spray cans poised
in our distress calling out
to the body

of Providence

sums,

building blocks,
rusty containers for the collected water
where the old float discarded,
fished by the young.

White '76 TR7

There was a white '76 TR7 for sale in the driveway
of a trailer house across the street,
and my imagination watered
with every look over my shoulder,
storm doors opened to a hole in the ground,
a gutted bird that I descended into,
Japanese Stratocaster in hand, my only asset,
salivation conditioned by a fantasy
in which I wrenched the car back to mint
and drove around nights
light streaked and soundtracked, fleshed in neon.

I didn't know anything about cars
and had no money
but I was born to live like the euphoric scrawl above a urinal
and I did, selling Smiths covers
with my hips and half of the chord changes,
aglow with greed for the world and an internal distortion
that squelched
when we lost that basement rehearsal space
and I watched the Triumph
squatting in goose grass and dandelions,
recede in the rearview
of my parent's Ford Fairmont for the last time.

Sometimes I Google 'White '76 TR7' but it's no good
having it now that it's possible —
desirability is a coefficient of need:
what I needed then was substance,
not because I had nothing but because I was nothing.

I don't pine for a body anymore,
but I do root around occasionally
for that broken string rusted of the moment,
a tug like the thump of a bass drum beater when I find it,
to sing along remembering the words,
please, please, please let me get what I want this time.

Warp

I have a copy of Gordon Lightfoot's *Summer Side of Life*
that I found in a thrift shop.
There's a skip near the end of "Cotton Jenny"
but I don't mind getting up
to move the needle past it.

She'll tell the story after knowing you minutes
about how her son died.
Some of her rooted then
and the part in motion tore away, continued.

That running woman looks over her shoulder a lot.
Sometimes she stumbles.
No one notices,
but she feels then as if she has to explain.
I don't mind the wringing of the dead child;
it's a service, once you're used to it,
same as scratched vinyl;
our world artlessly, accurately, described
again and again and again.

Japanese Ice Cream

In the dream I don't remember
but woke up thinking
put the deer repellant on the Hosta.
How I usually wake up, making lists.

I wrote you today, by pen,
remembering the relative intimacy
of recognizing, here and there,
my grandmother in her handwriting

thinking maybe someday
you'll re-read the letter
and that contact
will be worth something to me wherever I am.

Even the dick and balls
on the side of a boxcar is an altar call.

I complained to you
that no one burns wood anymore —
all pellet stoves and propane
bought from a box store
when 10 cords of white oak
is rotting into the ground
other side of the fence
from the Hosta I'm protecting.

Remember the old paper mill?
That smell so far from a fresh sheet of paper.
One thing doesn't have to follow another.

I didn't tell you to mind steep grades,
the shaded bits where ice
sleeps under a thin sand blanket
or to pay more for a UV resistant tarp.
What you get for not asking: bit rot.
The world can't be rice sweet

Disappearing by the Math

if you've used your front teeth even once
to skin the frosting from a Little Debbie.

How to be of a part with the tarp
and the ballcap on the dash -
eventually the way gives, efficacy declines,
grace yields to gravity, peels from the billboard.

If I voice my love enough I'll mean it,
proclaim meaning enough I'll love it.
What Bly said, "to leap out of misery
once or twice, and then back into the sea."

Tree frogs whitened on the gray
4x4 mailbox post, true sweet:
not advertising,
being, a shade off.

Put the flag up and leave my truth
on its back contemplating
the ceiling of the cave
and walk past the Hosta,
for over twenty years reliant on our care,
what will be eaten with us,
when we've quit waking to lists.

Back in the kitchen
mochi incubating in the freezer light
subtle reward,
for making a record.

Every Shelter in Place

Lest we forget how
(under desks when I was a kid,
now in sign-designated break areas
stocked with water and protein bars)
to hide
and outgunned, outnumbered, outwitted
as a flattened, trembling rabbit,
rake an ineffective nail at nothing worse
than what you know to be coming.

Today is a drill,
not the end of the world,
although some day it will be.

Someday the Western World will be secretly pleased
to have nothing to do, finally - no plans, expectations
just the diesel of doom, sweet as bedtime.

Someday while taking groceries from the car,
or adjusting column widths in a spreadsheet
or walking in circles after a run, hands on hips huffing
we'll hear the world say,

I just thought ...
It's my own fault ...
I should know better ... and sigh.

And then there will no longer be a need
to envision a future
in which we have attained satisfaction
with the moment
because the moment will be briefly,
all that there is: a door
pulled slowly closed to latch
on every shelter in place.

Snail Rider

a near perfect hole
maybe ragged once and proportioned
by routing insects, wind, rain
in the middle of the trunk
in the middle of the tree.

An eye in the stalk
as if the hump of the woods was shell
and underneath it
the mush of snail
moving, but slow as to be still
as standing at a window,
staring at a scarred tree,
holding the day back like a pulling dog.

Thinking maybe it began as a scrape
a succumbed sibling
reaching on the way down
unaccountable now
as anything but art.

The way it reflects me back to me
telling the strain
of squinting after a destination
beyond observation.
telling the grain,
mine, a snail rider.

Stone Boat

The first spiderweb walked through,
mid-August, sudden smell of a burrow,
winter dog-crawling, nosing into Summer.
A snail shell on a porch step, sun bleached
the kind of fetish I'd have kept as a kid
with other things awash in the volume of time
and stinking of after-magic.
Some rubbed and traced, carried off in mind
like the diving dress propped in a corner
of a Beach Haven curio shop that described the sea
with canvas, brass, rubber and glass so effectively
that I wore the idea of it home and refused to take it off,
descending away from summer's hot breath,
cutting firewood, pop flies to left field,
and once when I was 12, a girl, Lori Hawk.
Even her name a small, fierce, inscrutable urge.
Who I had arranged to meet,
passing a note from seat to seat on the bus.
The plan was to slip from my bedroom window
at first light but when I woke
to see her walking up and down the street
I lost my nerve,
lay in bed until I heard my father making coffee,
same relief as the third out of the ninth inning,
diving release
down to a joy I wouldn't know was practice until later,
exploring the deep for a shape to reply
to each season's sticky, common ask.
I've long grown out of the suit, the sea,
every other element, out of my hands and thumbs.
Now the seasons come without asking;
my father is gone, and with him went the stone boat
of cordwood overloaded on rusted springs,
rotted valve stems, and bald tires;
no more ballast, nothing to stop me rising,
using the door to walk out to meet Winter,
Spring, Summer, and Fall.

A Theory

It's on my lips to say
you not knowing
why you can no longer stand
looking to me
for an explanation well
remember when you were figuring out the road
and I held my breath
as if holding yours
lungs filled like sheets on a line,
the fresh bedding of a selective next breath,
a sleep and a wake up —
how my mother would count down
to vacation or Christmas.
When the tire crunched past
close enough to burn your nose,
hot rubber, asbestos, the screaming atoms
of impossibly foreign things
your body then turned you
to adrenaline and hackles,
which subsiding emptied you
of every desire
but to sleep and wake up.

See, it's a matter of maintaining morale
for dumb animals,
what I was about to call us
not unkindly.

A Response to Pablo Neruda

This morning at a four way stop
another car and I arrived at the same time
so I delayed braking
to provide proof to that other driver
that they were first to stop
and so could pull away.

As they did, the passenger waved
to let me know that she knew
that I had done them a kindness
and I thought yes this is better
than *stroking, raining words*,
and remembered you reaching for a small leaf
in the water by the bow of our canoe;
it floated just beyond and then past
until I reached an oar beneath it,
pear yellow bleeding to washed out red,
and offered it to you on the blade.

You took it in your fingers,
and then let it go to bounce in the wake,
letting me know that you understood
that I had handled
the *white hills, white thighs* of the mundane
with care, *body of my woman*
not corruptible by season or thirst
of silver-tongued devils.

Starting Over

A hair bird nest like a turned, wooden bowl
grounded beside a wheel of the grass-stained mower
reminds me that I have not been uniquely failed
by the belief that the future can be engineered
strand by strand, the way that I was certain
once that my chest, arms, and legs were inspired,
running behind a similar machine, wheels bouncing,
hurrying to earn an allowance between peels of thunder,
       pushing from chore to leisure
        - a borrowed car, borrowed girl -
borrowed mannerisms, hand in pocket fondling a roll
of sweat-damp bills I made myself,
carried home and arranged to spruce up the waiting
Which at that time was the excitement of changing air;
nothing yet arrived, survived, no refugee's walk
to a new place with similar chores
and the same, impetuous weather;
nothing new but the suspicion that a future is better told
by mute, empty nests and broken, hollowed eggs
than seconds added between combustions.

A hand on the starter cord, what I'd like:
to doubt that I am special,
to perform chores as ends in themselves,
to sit through old lessons content
that satisfaction isn't aggregate, can't be wooed,
obeys the physics I imagine.

The Songwriter

There wasn't enough art in loving anyone
so I bicycled to the inlet to sit beneath the Crepe Myrtles,
stalking each room of the house I played waiting for
an overlooked space to remind me of songs I owned to sing.

Sometimes a bicycle tire spun lazily in the breeze,
an off time beat to chiming, random domestic sounds nearby
which ticked like a dream of childhood, cooling.

I watched the shadow of my pencil track across a page
note by note until loosed by a sudden consonance
I'd reach for my bike and pedal home humming that melody
yet coming down, fretting it's worth, so that by the time
I dropped my bag and keys, everyone would have to rush
to make the believer's sign, collapse my doubt.

The inlet filled and sucked, filled and sucked.
The mud left after the water receded, smelled like birth,
whereas morning was life and noon death and evening
a kind of afterlife: what I stared into at the end of every day,
from a cloud of cigarette smoke on the fire escape,
trying to make the best of ambiguous meaning
while paying rent and gas.

There wasn't enough art in loving anyone but I tuned
to their dissatisfaction, certain that theirs were the songs in me.
I never wondered why it was I thought it right
that ownership was prize for guessing the value of suffering.
Yet I can't dislike myself then, that boy stretched
in the fine Atlantic sun, sure that his innocence
was experience, that art forgives. I keep him close,
still the operator of my dirty work
whenever I meet someone whose song I want to sing.

To Loneliness

We've become too hard maybe
to love death in earnest outright
and deaths everywhere wait around
below windows, hands in pockets
alone at the arrivals gate,
at the end of the bar with a fake number.

What we do so as not to give ourselves
to whatever wants us
to remain cutting ourselves
with the razor of self-awareness.

Why not gamble
on the terrible beauty of anonymity?
No language, just death swiped right,
nothing serious, no commitment,
the only ask a shared glance, walk,
on the sidewalk, in the Walmart.

Sensitive Boy

Though we have ice cream trucks, Bic lighters,
bicycles, jazz, and the pentatonic scale
it's maddening how I've imagined myself
in the reflection of this controlled experiment
as reliable, well-designed and productive,
that generations from the onboarding
I still perceive the moon in its window,
stars on their grooved tracks,
my daughter and wife curled
into intersecting dreams
as genius rather than script,
lie staring at the time listening
to the air blowing through the duct work
of the ship, the biosphere,
scientists at that moment pressing their faces
against the blacked-out windows
trying to see into the weedy lot beyond.

If ferns and horseshoe crabs
have existed 300 million years
then surely I can learn to sleep
while time watches, find peace
within the boundaries of my shape.
I don't want to be awake, circling,
feeling the walls for the outline of a door
The human story should be enough:
money, Velcro, sneakers, espresso,
crosswalks, homeless encampments,
sunroofs, romance, Jesus but I'm tired
of looking at myself, of being the sensitive boy.
Is it just me that can't coalesce?
Who will wake up at home in this place,
not wanting to build somewhere else
from the parts of it?

Linear Increase

It's humiliating, the pang
for the passing of the stewardship of parenthood,
for scuffed time,
but this is more the tension of a go-live,
of drafting paper, gum erasers,
the hot plastic air of processor fans.

The starlings are flying counter-clockwise,
      I have a hangnail,
You found a glass broken in the dishwasher.
When can we expect to see some data?

Now a salamander is climbing the gate.

Remember when Sarah dumped her truck
into the ditch at the end of the driveway?
She just slammed it into four wheel and gunned it,
lurched away in a gravel asteroid field.

The Black Rhinoceros is extinct.
Some crazy percentage of biodiversity
is disappearing every day.

Her rabbit was eaten by a coyote.
Her Guinea pig got scurvy.
Time is passing,
and we don't know any more now,
beneath the swaying umbilical
of phone, security lights
than when she was born,
a bear blocking the road home from the hospital
watching us paused,
mouthing our fear to each other.

Self-Harm at the Outlet Mall

You are looking for a sundress.
And it occurs to me.

A wet footprint retreating
between a dead chickadee and my sneaker,
grass straightening to the light,
a calm spot in the chop of water rippling toward
Old Navy, Lululemon, Ann Taylor.

Not in the rain, after,
in the steam of returning heat.

I'm glad to be here with you.
But this country is all teeth.
I'm tempted to lie down next to the bird,
tell time with it,
be the guy who's fucks flew off,
that the world walks wide around.

It's obvious, despite the signage,
that we are most real in the nose.

I can't be the only one
carrying sad luck like a fidget toy,
distracting my mind
with motor commands
while the world sucks the evidence
of my being back up into the sky.

I don't want to give up on you,
or finding your sundress,

I just have to believe
That it's normal to be tempted
to cut a thin cold moment in the heat,
to allow my eyes to catch rain,
and despair that living won't allow it.

Goldfinch

A break in the traffic pushed me
away from the cigarette butts,
plastic bags, sneakers,
things lost their fight at the bus stop
to fly across the road
winged, nose squashed but
fists balled and grinning split lips
asking for it again,
      the insult
         "Pretty boy,"
spat at me a second time
confirmation of the first, no accident.

Pinned by the shadow
of his sleeveless, muscled anger
lengthening my own in the cinders, blood,
hot wash of exhaust,
I had the premonition
that it would be worth having dared him
to get off at my stop
just to be able to warble that boast,
      "Pretty,"
long and jumbled
to each day thereafter,
and I have, often,
living up to the standards
of that cocky bird.

My Father Paints Us a New Car

Shirtless, bandanna'd,
squatting split old loafers in the dandelion mined gravel
applying faculty to need,
eyeballing the seams,
flattening waves of Bondo with a folded piece of sandpaper.
Sun freckling his shoulders,
inhaling the paint while he worries each stroke,
picks at bits of leaf and pollen blown into the wet,
aware of the wind. He stands back,
watches shadows of leaves play on a fender,
a dapple of confidence and certainty of failure
that he squints away,
blurring the rust into like-new,
Sears Hunter Green livening the driveway quartz
like creeper a dead tree.

Remembering as if already happened
his wife's hand on the pitted chrome,
opening the door and settling
into the dry vinyl and off-gassing paint,
a stray glossy bristle breaching a quarter panel implying
that her man can provide whatever she is willing to accept
as good enough, valued beyond
whatever handicap she has set for her gratitude,
that weight pulling at the corners of her optimism,
as determined to see a win as he is to ignore her doubt.

The Phenomena

Your boots by the door
in the morning sun
loudly recall fiddleheads,
mud, a blooming pear tree,
the thin, bone-cool fingers of your hand
until you kneel to tie the laces,
then my perception begins to trundle,
knock and thunk,
a soft analog noise canceling
any sense of you.

I have to be alone
with insensate things like your boots
to recall you,
the trail,
the still sharp cut grass,
direction, time.

Even the dog that charged us
        barking,
stopped, pricked ears, veered away
as if from a phenomena
out of place,
flaring my distrust of clarity.

Hides

Sort light mid dark pile hip the basket
in the smell of what happened
yesterday earlier in the week
and of who

down the stairs to the machine
to watch my face in the soap-streaked washer door
always losing a boy's game of comparison
to whatever, everything better
stared at from my truck in passing
through the dog-snotted window

This morning a coyote,
unconcerned, fat,
pelt like frozen salt foam,
like snow on sand,
trotting purposefully through a break in a hedgerow.

First time I stayed the night
I borrowed a clean shirt from your brother
It smelled like your detergent
which was the smell of you until I'd undressed you

First time I undressed you
you had cut your leg on a sharp chair in seminar
I was first to respond.

Now I carry your skin like a chore
shaking my old horns at briars of habit.
Now I keep coagulate at hand
which is not the same as being unprepared but able.

I'd like for my blood to rise again
scenting you in these dirty clothes;
your blood to glue me to your side
just because it's your body

A few days back I found a note on a pasture gate,

'Will trap your coyotes,' and a phone number
I texted him and said no thanks,
they weren't bothering anything.
"Not yet," he said. "Call me when they do."

Bits of his note, left in a pocket,
snow from the dried clothes
as I carry them up the stairs
silencing the complaining wood, nails
as if I was weightless
reminding me that walking

spites prophecies, confounds theft:
to move in your owned hide
in the meantime of your habitat
without a look back or around
is lived-in love, not briars.

Open Carry

A dogwood petal lands on a sleeve,

a starling angles just so as to brush a bare shoulder.

Why do we shrug when the world comforts itself?

It's as good as a caress of the limbs we used to have.

This dude at the feed store eyed my look as if a curse

and reached to touch the grip of a Glock

to ward off the uncertainty of my intention.

All I can think, the ugly butt of that metal

how good it feels in the hand

maybe as good as the weight of petals, birds.

Flip the visor to that little vanity mirror

and see a glint,

maybe energy singing in the dark,

a song in your eye

about the terrible softness of our bodies.

For Albert Hawkins
(Whom the State Has Labeled a Hoarder)

His works and wonders are pennies to wedge into each blown fuse to keep the lights on at any cost. A fire trap, what they will say, not seeing the house for the acrid tendrils of what if, the collection of doors like trailheads, rooms natural wonders.

As if moderation could be at home, when home is a bottomless word.

But that, and that, and that call a question so nearly right that surely some next thing will be the what that knows what to ask, each query an acquisition of a mote, dinner eaten above the bedrock answer on a scavenged table made three legged by ankle threatening regolith.

What birth doesn't sore the eyes, isn't terrible? His squalling rust, rot, mildew: energies decoding our promise beneath the escaped, writhing byproduct of that combustion: a snow of old receipts, newspapers, yellowed mail, steel, glass, plastic, rubber; the whiskered, nicotined shoveler sweating shirtless before the furnace.

Look at yourself as you pass by, there in the hoarder Albert Hawkins.

Golden Boys

The tanned, squint lined bodies that rang of weather
sang like boys in adventure books swimming naked
knife in teeth parting the kelp with fish belly fingers
bodies slippery deboned of every care but curiosity
ever finding themselves the barest outline
emerging from a camouflage in the hallway
metal banging of locker doors, macaque cries,
swooping parrots.

I held a jackknife gilded black
against the grainy love of their jaunty smiles
until rafted pitching and yawing
on the square of my bedroom window
I descended the rough knots
and fled buoyancy for consoling pressure
not as if I had never been an animal but as if
I had never not been darting joy
I finned, forgot the mimed wrestling, nipping,
huffed oxygen from the water wondering
at the availability of the stuff
lusted after at library reading tables
leaking a slime confounding the impulse to walk,
that parasite inherited from my land bound mother
but unknown to the school of golden boys
at the bottom of the lake waiting,
kicking at the gravel, leaning on handlebars
who welcomed me into the fidelity of the precise measure
of the space between me and the boy I followed,
myself and the boy following me.

Lover

The stars watch, same as your face
in the lit kitchen window.
You looking back at yourself looking away
to open the gate, unlatch the bin.
Face like a little moon, with its own gravity,
pulling, adjusting.
A flash of panic when you lose yourself
and relief, sliding from between the trees.

Gazing from a puddle,
which love is that, your expression?
What happens when you fall for yourself,
when you lie down next to your voice:
every moment a roll call
waiting for the reply
        voiced as a pinhole of light,
immediately retreating
as if embarrassed at having made that sound.

Place the bottle on the others, latch the bin.
Close the gate, hold still as
the energy of glass on glass flattens,
you somehow with it,
less than even a shadow
in the shadow abundant suburbs until

a screech owl whinnies
faintly in the circle of outer dark
so alien as to cause you to recall yourself
and with leaping pulse recognize your lover
distorted on the door of the neighbor's car,
the winking, geometric light
of that bird described
just enough to flesh you.

Yield

I didn't want to change state.

I saw the shadow of your hand reaching and

I wanted my time.

I don't understand chemistry,

how something can break down and become sweeter.

Only you guessed how I'd taste past the skin.

What was I before you caused me to ripen?

What do I call myself now that I have?

Pop Song

These eggs that I wash every morning
before tucking them into the carton
remind me of washing my daughter

no less carefully, with an eye to the future
knowing her cost and improbability.

Like stroking a pocket rabbit's foot,
thumb stopping
on the sharp bone beneath the fur:

the luckiest things are the least likely.

Roll an egg in your palm:
it's a spirit level finding true.

Once, stumped around a friend's deathbed,
a nurse suggested some music to pass to.

I think of that phrase, humming
to the radio above the hens squawking,
winners to date, praising.

When You Stretch I

1.

feel the breeze tousling
an orchard waiting for a keeper,
your quivering muscles readying
for a day's work worrying
your reliability like lead keeping
the yellow-jacket wing
of my fragile optimism
from the shake of your daily climb
through knobbed, scratching suckers
up the use-shined ladder
leant against time sounding
the mattress with waves repeating
history, history to come.

2.

feel the shake of your daily climb
up a use-shined ladder
leant against my optimism
tousling the jangly suckers,
buzzing my fruit, your wing noise
a resined, horse-hair sigh
that the keeper is coming.

Dressed for the Flood

Where is the water in your eyes?
It's in everyone's.
Yours are flatlands, cap rock, arroyo.
The soft dirt that implies a life in water past.
Your eyes keep miracles of adaptation
in sand crevasses, beneath overhangs,
clever, efficient oddities
that live on secretions dependent on variables
felt not understood;
and so you are attuned, drought

dressed for the flood,
waves eroding water,
your desert, no wonder
for the sea grass, for the swimmer.

Idiom

A middle-aged man dressed
for work leaning
into an open passenger
window and a woman leaning

toward him from the driver's
seat so that
the two of them form a
truss, her hand extended,

fingers stretched to press
flat on the mussed head presented
and held for a moment,
the bliss of touch stripping

the everyday from it.
A simple embrace
of the gravity
of watching the other erased

by the limits of vision.
That could be us, throwing
the sign of ourselves like
an apotropaic eye

at the chaos curbside;
you and me a peculiar culture,
speaking figures gawked
at the Kiss & Ride.

The Unknown

A puzzle of load, stress.

A thicket of determined safe keeping.

A cage of branches, twigs,
shy, busy suckers gathering creeper,
maintaining posture to deflect
any attempt to read an approach
from signs, themselves tangles,
traps spring loaded,

irreducible complications armed
above light stippling moss,
boulders like new bread,
bass sunning in the shallows.
A question hanging:

Should I wake you?
Will you want to be touched?

Fetch

My first act
before I knew what I was

A reflex, really,
deflecting the incoming
thing

Humid,
       gnat clouded

the texture of a caw.

The sticky, shark skinned
side of a blade of grass

The whistling side

Which makes me think it was that whistle
and not the slobbery lacrosse ball
       rolling into the ivy
that flushed the word into the open.

I didn't know then not to chase it.

Always just in back of
I fetched myself to it
again and again
until I tripped
and it came sniffing

I thought it a neat trick,
but it turns out that curiosity
       is opposite empathy

and you only have so much to lose.

So come, no reward.

Every Morning Song

The way morning air is peeled, chewed,

cored, pinched, pulped,

skins like blown plastic bags, petals snowing the rain

cradled by, snagged in burying disquiet;

the way we sang,

discarded beer bottles rain-filled just right

at the dump. Each thing called its name

winged from the backs of pickups, upended, emptied.

Names that sparrowed

while we lanked around after the glint of wings,

cages at the ready.

The air the same air as this, decades later:

singing tetanus and treasure

voicing and listening for a reply.

Rosslyn Plaza

*For the Woman who sits every day
in Rosslyn Plaza by McDonald's*

Our tripping hearts
Can't comprehend the drag
Of rooted awareness sitting
In a chair on the plaza watching
Us being born, living full lives or not
Growing old and dying and
She still the mountain being,
Layered sweatpants, shorts,
Socks, hoodies.
Overlooking the plaza
Occasionally sleeping and
When she wakes she is ever taken
Aback by the span revealed the
Colors, stratifications,
Movement of the terrain indicating
Forces still doggedly working.
And surprised, always, that she is not
Alone in black space weightless
In a vacuum the way
She knows she will
Surely one day be remaining
After in the quiet
Abandoned even
By the fluttering instants
Of childhood, everything
Peeled to the speck
before the clod and stone,
Matter undeniably
transient beneath the weather.

Naturalization

We sneakered the path daily
between paused bulls
and the Norfolk-Southern

jerking, riprapped wheels balanced
on a shriek mussing our hair.
Joked ourselves hoarse

passing through the milkweed
to the culvert, where, impressed by
our poverty of experience

we crewed an imagined ship
stinking of boys
begging freedom from the sea.

Now at the wheel of return
I begin to say,
my eye catching on the grass,

shivering above the culvert
as if with the persistence
of my longing then,

"This is where,"
but the green words
are dust without the accent

and there's no way
I will allow myself
the risk of that twang now.

Give

The pet rabbit was screaming,

limp in the teeth of the young setter

whose jaw trembled, leaked drool

to be so close to what nature demanded

and yet having learned the utility

of a soft mouth yielded

and sat beside you in the grass;

a good dog.

That memory is in my ear

as I dodge your reach for my collar,

carrying a squealing argument,

the need to win wound in the memory of an urge

to lie down in some space of my own

and tear the throat and gut from us,

when what I want is your hand

patting the grass beside you, asking, "sit."

Banyan

Argue the knot, sound,
by the predictable rotation,
familiar funk, sun
flecked shoes cast off,
some dogged time for neither nor.

Where shadow asks slowly
and the not present inhabit
our cast-off clothes lounging
the hours left to be naked,

rafted, drafting near nothing
above the plats, surveys, pins,
traffic crying the hazards we mimic
making fun.

Buoys on the parallels,
as many as there are loves.
They make light work.

Canopy Shyness

She conducts the sound of bristles working.
Pacing, looking out of the window,
scrubbing each small quadrant
as if searching for a body.
She selects, examines,
and then carefully replaces
this random thing or that.
Lifts her top, leans back,
looks at her belly in the mirror.
Turns side to side appraising
and drops the hem,
squats, stands, squats;
maybe a set of ten.
Wags from the room
and lifts, examines,
replaces in other rooms.
Sings through the buzz,
makes her way into the bathroom.
Turns on the tap, spits, rinses, spits again.

There is an oak tree in the yard
grown up beside its sister,
so close as to touch but won't.
Why I watch,
the breadth of love apart
from her moving shy of me.
I keep that measure,
a lucky number,
space for the symbiotic things
to flit back and forth between us.
But beneath the thump of her heel to toe
in that close nature
our reach knits
and absent mind we fill each the other's lack;
the familiar voice of that activity
the sound of her moving through the house,
now watering the plants.

Driving Home From a Funeral, Solving For X

It reminded me in a peripheral way
of the motel room,

how we were delayed back to ourselves
in near real time
by your inverse self kited,
snapped like a sheet,
bumping the ceiling

gusted up there
by a pair of headlights at the intersection

arresting your form
and our attention
like hot air cooled by a shade tree
or a dawn lit rabbit ear,

and then wrecked,
no different than her sudden displacement,

one day a sack of water treading water
coaxing her dog into a Kentucky lake,
chin lifted for a kiss,
the next flattened

into a photograph of the same
in a vestibule smelling of Presbyterians.

She's three dimensional now
only on my skin,
an emulsion
still hipping the light of her arms and legs
silvered by childhood,
weightless as salt.

A single, tangled thought
that continued while driving home past Camden Yards

Disappearing by the Math

equally vacant and inky,
energies retreated each to nest,
the mechanics of that orientation
the same old secret

(
If I only knew how much the lake had risen
    when she waded into it
        to hold the figure of her volume ...

    a reliable hurt
        implies a quantitative comfort
)

Do I remember your ring size?
I used to know it.

I know your height, weight,
the three words of your name.

All of the numbers and proper nouns
that hem the doubt walking
just beyond reach of my faith.

So it was with a pilgrim's certainty
that I arrived at the home I expected,
and woke the next morning to the sun
looking for and then finding your shape

to send it pooling with my own,
a deeper black solving for X,
where X is the tangible you,

holding the fact of your figure
in the tangled hedge of our rising,
against your possible outcomes,
the variable of my happiness.

Fire Break

No combustion fingering the fuel reaching just

a pause on the flat low, mergansers brushed

on the thinnest top measure of water.

Urine splashing our toes, dizzying Canaan down the road.

Pitching and rolling, each with a hand

on the thing we burst from, holding ourselves

at the low middle. Dutifully maintaining

the fire break, carefully aiming,

staring straight ahead, begging the natural forces.

What / Nothing

A photo
of dogs long gone

To look at it is to feel
the furred skin sled
over fat and ribs

Dead dogs looking lively
at the down on your cheek:
what / nothing,
your question / my answer,
accidentally true.

True Romance

Standing in front of the window
reflected back as if in the Cypress tree beyond,

myself behind you in the room
books, mail on the desk,

laptop light like an opening in each of us
pebbled in condensation,

you there and me back here,
queued same as always, speleothems,

each a stretched bounce.
So much that moves us we won't ever sense.

Why did we make the bed, again and again,
cultivating that wildness?

A strategy of occupation
shunting the periodic table,

all leg and belly.
What a joke

to find that romance is the prudish thing
and the elements swing from the ceiling.

Oh, it makes us laugh now,
a spooned tone that some mistake for nothing

still sure that sediment is dumb.

Yellow Boy
(uncountable, slang) Iron (III) hydroxide, a yellow-orange solid found in acidic water from mining projects

I thought I had invented
that way of lying
against the current

so that the water like hands
cupped my shoulders
palmed my head

an element
owning me
as itself.

Bedded on bladderwort
I hosted mating wheels
fed the nibbling fry

everything suggested
that I was of a part

How tragic then it seemed
to harden and flake

to have to choose between
        dissolution
and the river.

Atlas

The star always in the same pane, third from the left
like a box it's kept in is nothing, probably
just travel exhausted light but gutters on regardless.
The wonder it stokes

in my small, animal imagination is a close, warm, space
in the dark when the sound of my heart expanding and collapsing
seems more house noise than bodily function.
What constellation is that,

the story of the stop between beats?
A clock is watched in expectation but stars are watched
to see what's been; not till, past. In the pauses between
sleep cycles they,

in their dogged runs, lull us into assuming that
today's experience is tomorrow's promise.
Which is what I'm doing now, watching remembered morning
turn the redbud suckers thin and bright as crazes in glass,

anticipating morning while night lasts,
which is what night does,
a sightless day for our kind anyway.
How cold the black around the star looks
and funny how often smallness causes us to imagine ourselves large,

like looking at a distant mountain and pinching it between fingers;
or lying now in bed imagining I'd like to grow giant size
and stride out of the house and down this hill
which is itself a pinched remnant.

But even giant, I know I'd be just a small thing
keeping still within a larger shape
like the center of a crow in the rain.
Smallness is of a course for a thing born
where there is more nothing than anything.

Disappearing by the Math

This bed is commonplace and warm with promise,
a given name in a clutter of unsigned things,
a kind of public recording and I feel claimed
if by nothing but needs temporarily met
and the sweet pop of vertebrae adjusting.

When I close my eyes I see my atoms arrayed,
my own emitting light, my own distant sisters;
like me not burning but radiating effort,
shouldering the order of things.

Sometimes I wake in the memory of a long-gone intimacy
and that star and I are bound like that, coinciding for a while
and then separated by degrees,
following momentum through the matter
of the hundred billion souls scaffolding Atlas.

But that's tomorrow's work. Tonight
I'll watch time pass until it slips beyond the window frame,
and stall, bed in my senses while I can.

Acknowledgments

Thank you to the editors and readers of the journals and magazines that first housed these poems, including: *Avalon Literary Review, Cleaver Magazine, The Wild Word, Hiram Poetry Review, Grand Little Things, Bear Paw Arts Journal, Stick Figure Poetry Quarterly, Dreamstreets, EKL Review, Poetry Life & Times, The Insurgence, Plato's Caves, Galway Review, Backwards Trajectory, Beltway Poetry Quarterly, Bluepepper, River Heron Review, Dunes Review, Hampden-Sydney Review, Killing the Buddha, Triggerfish Critical Review, Tiny Seed Literary Journal,* and *Spellbinder Magazine.*

Special thanks to the chemical elements Carbon, Hydrogen, Nitrogen, Oxygen, Phosphorus, and Sulfur, tattooed on my arm and without which we living organisms would not exist. Thanks to Algebra, Physics, Biology, Geology, Cartography, and Chemistry; all subjects that I failed in school but have since discovered as The Way. Thanks to Michelle, my love story, Arwen to my Aragorn, Nerds 4 Life. Thanks to our daughter Autumn, faster, smarter, and stronger that we are. Thanks to my teachers who many years ago taught me to think like a writer: Dr. Ed Jones, William Miller, and Colin Falk. Thank you to my parents for creating me, even though I explained many times as a teenager that I never asked them to do it. Thanks to John Craig for his pot-reeking attic of wonders and for *Rundy's Journal*. Thanks to Peter Craig for sharing his love of literature and being, as was his father, my always interested and enthusiastic booster. Thanks to Jennifer Yeatts and Aly Allen for their careful reading of the manuscript and contribution of reviews for the cover. Thanks to Candice James and Silver Bow Publishing for taking a chance on me and this book. Thanks to Bob Dorsey, the Nitro in my Funny Car. Thanks to all the dogs and horses that have been good and true friends. Thanks to the Susquehanna, Shenandoah, and Potomac rivers and Lakes Huron, Superior, and Michigan. Thanks lastly to the beautiful places I call home: DC, the Shenandoah Valley, Traverse City, Marquette, and Philadelphia.

Author Profile

Matt Thomas is a smallholder farmer, engineer, and Pushcart Prize nominated poet. His poetry has appeared in *The Wild Word, Tiny Seeds Literary Journal, Avalon Literary Review, Bear Paw Arts Review, Triggerfish Review,* the *Hampden-Sydney Review, Hiram Review, Galway Review, Cleaver Magazine, River Heron Review, Dunes Review,* and elsewhere. *Disappearing by the Math* is his first book.

Matt received his MA in English from Old Dominion University where his research focused on rhetoric and technology. After graduating he started a software consulting company which began a thirty-year career in business software development and information technology. He published his first poem at age 50 and has published regularly since then. He and his family live in Virginia where they practice land conservation and stewardship in the historic Shenandoah Valley. They are glad denizens of DC, Philadelphia, Traverse City, and Marquette.

www.ingramcontent.com/pod-product-compliance
Lightning Source LLC
Chambersburg PA
CBHW070122110526
44587CB00017BA/3244